C000221000

Bodies, Babies and Bellybuttons!

by Lynnette Smith

Copyright © BigTalk Education. The right of Lynnette Smith to be identified as author of this work has been asserted in accordance with the Copyright Designs and Patents Act 1988. All rights reserved.

Published in the U.K. by:
BigTalk Education
Oakworth House
Althorpe
North Lincolnshire
DN17 3HJ
www.bigtalkeducation.co.uk
@BigTalkEd

Illustrations by Pat Carrington and Heidi Singleton

The publisher makes no representation expressed or implied with regards to the accuracy of the information contained in this book and cannot accept any responsibility or liability.

Except for the quotation of small passages for the purposes of criticism and review, no part of this publication may be reproduced, stored in a retrieval system, or transmitted, in any form or by any means, electronic, mechanical, photocopying, recording or otherwise except under the terms of the Copyright Designs and Patents Act 1988 without the prior consent of the publisher at the address above.

ISBN 978-0-9927840-2-7
Printed in the U.K. by Ashford Colour Press Ltd.

All content in this book is for the purpose of guidance, discussion and awareness only. No advise should be taken without making your own judgement or, in the case of serious problems seeking professional advice.

The Big Talk Made Easy

Preface

Why Start Early?

Because it's easier. Young children are fabulous, and as all parents know, they ask loads of questions. Not least of all about their bodies and your body. Most parents of pre-schoolers have no qualms about answering these; however, once they start school, parents seem to be more reticent, perhaps fearful of the response from teachers or other parents if the children share such knowledge. As a young child, they will accept the answers you give them without embarrassment or discomfort, because they trust you and they have yet to be fed with information from other children or the media.

Won't it take away their innocence?

Nothing takes away innocence quicker than sexual abuse. Knowledge about their bodies won't stop them wanting to fly kites, go sledging or make sandcastles. When body science is discussed they just add it to their knowledge bank; it's adults that try and keep it separate and make it such a big issue.

Children want their parents to be the first people to talk to them about their bodies, sex and relationships. Why would we want them to receive any of that information from someone else or via a dubious site on the internet? Safeguarding children through appropriate knowledge has to be our priority now more than ever before; with the advent of the internet, it is often easier to consult Google rather than a parent. Parents need to be proactive if they want to protect their children and provide a moral framework, passing on personal values as well as the biology.

Many parents want to do this but perhaps don't know where to start, what to say, how to say it and when to say it.

This book will help start the process. It guides you through the basics and it can be used as a storybook script with added insights for parents at the base of each page.

At the back are other topics and words which give an easy definition or explanation suitable for even young children. As the child grows the book can remain on their bedroom shelf for reference, for them and, very probably, their friends.

We're all individual; we're all different, and we are all special and unique.

Children need to know that they are loved and cared for; this encourages good self-esteem and helps build resilience against bullying, name calling, etc. To understand we are all different shapes and sizes can also help with body image issues.

PG

Nobody should hurt you; they shouldn't hit you, smack you or kick you. Who would you tell if they did?

PG

From a young age, children should know that their bodies are their own, and that other people shouldn't hurt them. It's good to identify at least two adults they would be happy to confide in, one at home and one outside the home – maybe at school or nursery.

Some families have different names for parts of our bodies, but if we think like scientists we can use the correct names then nobody gets confused or embarrassed.

Some parts of our bodies are private. Do you know where these parts are?

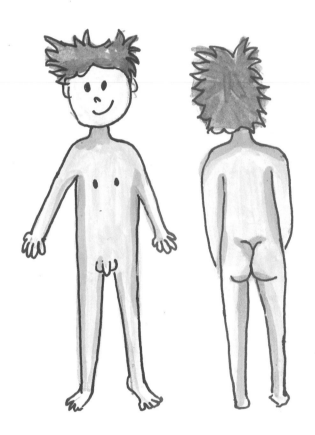
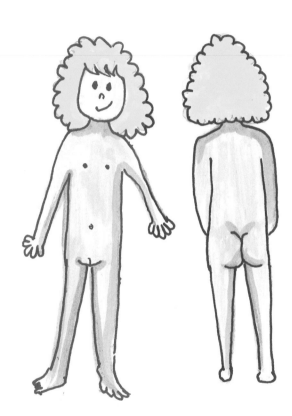

If your family has an 'open bathroom door' policy then children from a very young age will know there are differences between males and females. If you are happy with this then it is a very positive way for children to learn about differences and provides opportunities to ask questions.

PG

There are four parts which are private: our mouths, our chests, our genitals (that's the area between our legs; boys have penises, girls have vaginas), and our bottoms (or anus, which is the scientific word). Nobody should touch these unless we want them to, or make us kiss them if we don't want to.

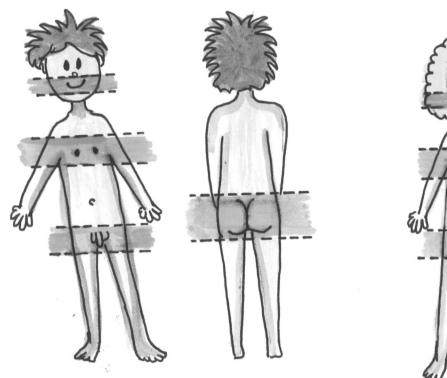

PG

It is really important that children know the correct scientific names for their genitals. In the event of them ever being inappropriately touched they have the vocabulary to give exact information. For example: "they touched my Minnie/Maryflower" is very vague, as opposed to "they touched my vagina". Child abusers prefer uneducated children – those who don't have the words and knowledge of what's right and wrong, or the ones who haven't had those conversations with a parent/carer and where the channels of communication aren't as clearly open for a child to raise their concerns.

We shouldn't touch other people's private areas either.

The amount of children touching other children inappropriately is rising. Children need to know that their body is private from anyone that they don't want to touch it, whether that is an adult or another child. They need reassurance that they must tell. Clarify that 'surprises' are okay; for example, birthday cakes or presents, but that secrets are not okay.

PG

It is okay for us to touch these parts of our body in private, in our bedroom or the bathroom. As we grow we might want to see or feel how our body is changing.

PG

It's normal for even young children to be curious about their bodies and want to touch and expose them. Encourage them to go to a private place if they want to do this. With small children distraction may be the best option in a public place; remember not to chastise, even if you feel embarrassed.

We shouldn't show them outside or let people take photographs of our private parts.

A good benchmark should be: if we did that action as an adult, would it be legal? Urinating or exposing our genitals, etc. in public can lead to fines or prosecutions.

PG

Now for some more body science.

Boys and girls can both do lots of things and many parts of their bodies are similar, but some parts are different. Our bodies need food and liquid to keep us healthy and to help us to grow. The body takes what it needs and gets rid of the waste. Solid waste comes out of our anus and liquid waste gathers in the bladder and comes out of our urethra. The boy's urethra is at the end of his penis. Boys have two openings.

bladder

anus

urethra

penis

PG Their bodies and bodily functions fascinate children. To explain the functions in a "body science" way makes sometimes embarrassing topics much easier to discuss.

Girls have an anus for solid waste too and the urethra is between their legs, but they also have another opening which makes three. The third opening is called a vagina; this is a tube which runs between the uterus and the outside of the body.

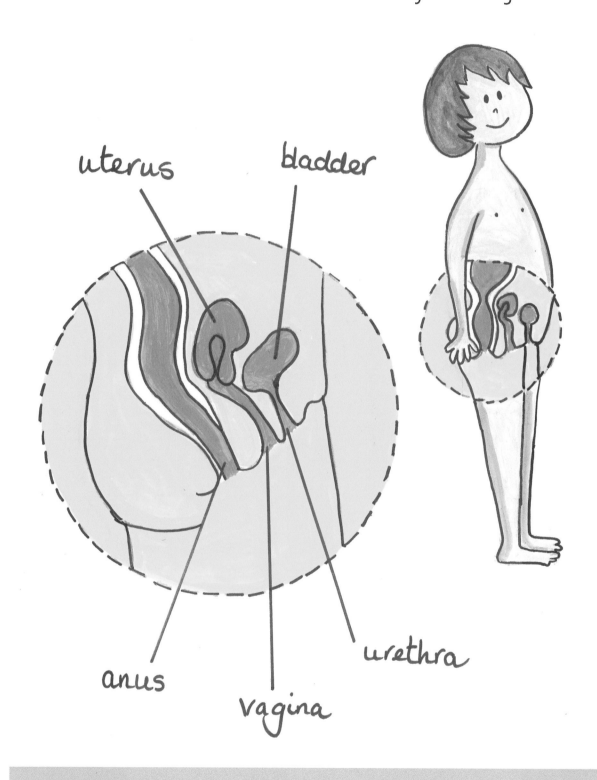

uterus

bladder

anus

vagina

urethra

This basic body science is invaluable. I have worked with teenagers and adults who have found this information very important, having never covered it at home or in primary school. As a result, when it came up at senior school, they were too embarrassed to listen or learn properly.

PG

It is important to look after our bodies; kicking or grabbing them can hurt and cause damage. It is also important to keep our bodies clean by washing them regularly.

PG *Children need to be aware that touching, grabbing or 'wedgies' (pulling the back of underpants or knickers) is not acceptable. It can be threatening, embarrassing and very painful, potentially causing harm to the genitals. Boys should be encouraged to wash their penis properly, especially around and under the foreskin, to ensure there is no build-up of smegma, which can cause infections.*

Boys have a small bag made of skin behind the penis called a scrotum.

In here are the testicles which produce two things: testosterone, which is the boy hormone, and when he is older, sperm.

These parts of our body are very important because we need them when we grow up and want to have children of our own.

When a man and a woman want to have a baby they need a sperm from the man; these are grown inside the testicles. Some children might call these 'balls'.

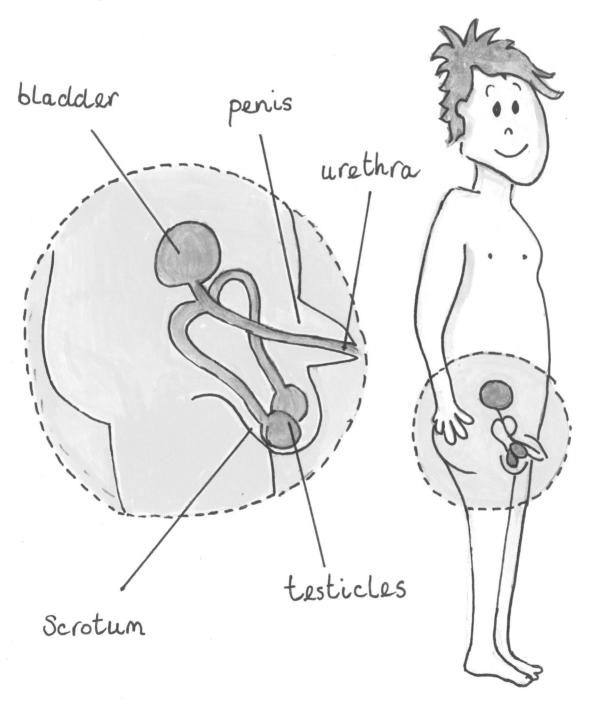

bladder

penis

urethra

Scrotum

testicles

Let's look at girls' bodies.

Like the boys, girls have 'balls' but they're on the inside. These are called ovaries; they produce oestrogen which is the girl hormone, and when she is older, the eggs (or ovum), which you need if you want to have a baby.

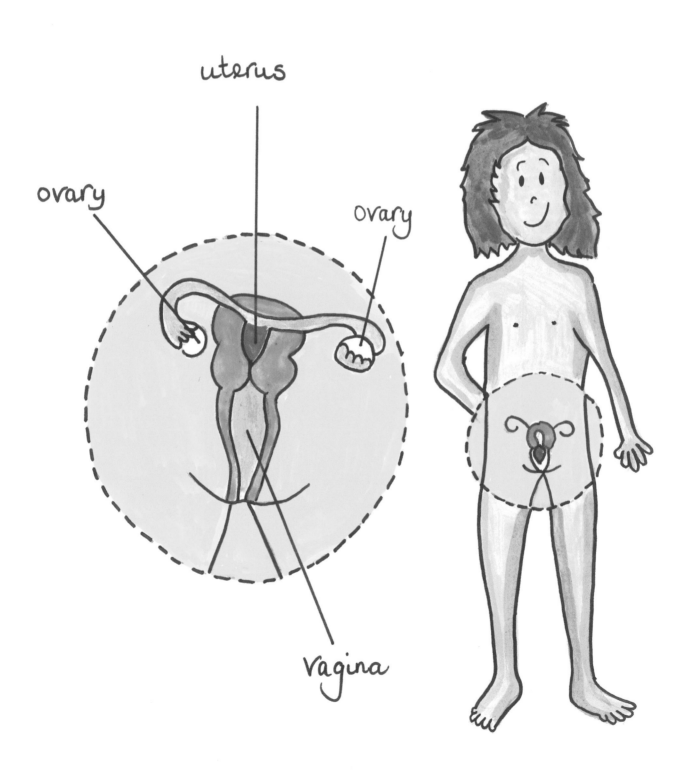

uterus

ovary

ovary

vagina

When adults love each other and want to make a baby they usually do this somewhere warm, cosy and private like in bed. They cuddle up close and the man's penis becomes erect which means it gets stiffer and grows a little in length. He is then able to gently place it inside the vagina so that the sperm can move across.

This is called "sex" or "having sex" but we like to call it "making love" as people only usually do this with someone they love, trust, respect and care for.

Some parents and carers fear talking to their children about sex for many reasons. Parents initially tell me they want to be their child's main sex educator but will want to wait until the child is ten or twelve. What they fail to realise is that although this meets their comfort needs, the child will have learned about sex way before then, often in a way that is rude and crude from either friends, peers, the media or numerous other sources.

PG

As the sperm from the man swims up the vagina it makes its way to the ovum, which has been released from the ovary. When the sperm meets the ovum they merge to make a foetus, which is the beginning of a baby.

The tiny baby starts to grow inside the womb; a tube from the mother passes all the food and liquid it needs. It floats around in a bag of water inside the womb; it's a safe place for it to grow until it is ready to be born.

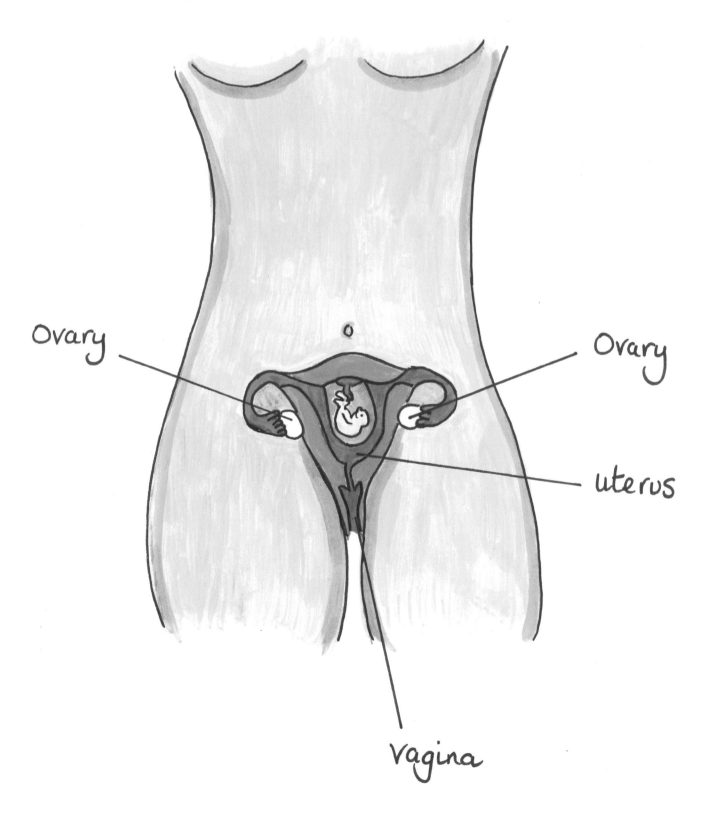

Ovary

Ovary

uterus

Vagina

The baby takes nine months to grow; each month it gets bigger until, eventually, it is ready to be born.

3 months   6 months   9 months

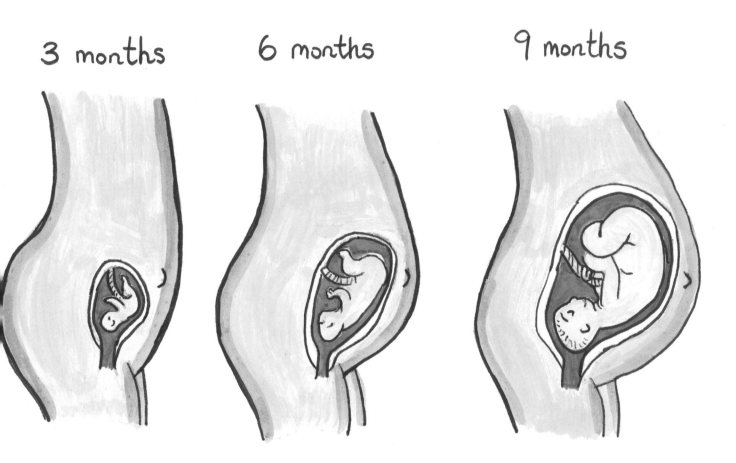

Many children are aware of women being pregnant and their tummies getting bigger. These pictures are useful for older siblings to track progress. Even primary age children are often aware of words like 'miscarriage' and 'abortion', usually picked up from the media or having overheard family discussions.

PG

When the baby has been in its mother's tummy for approximately nine months, the mother's body gets ready for it to be born. This is called labour.

The bag of water inside the womb, which has helped keep the baby safe, breaks open; the water rushes out, making it slippery, ready for the baby to be born. The cervix opens up just wide enough for the baby to be pushed out by the mother. It is a very exciting time.

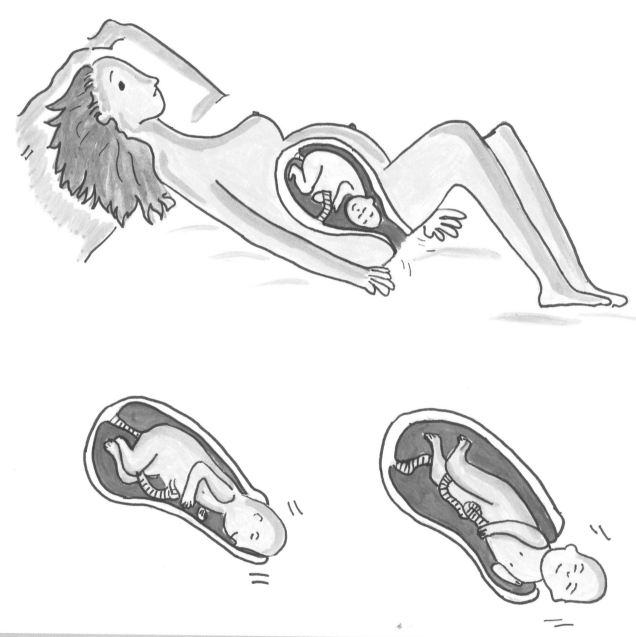

PG With the numerous programmes about pregnancy and birth now shown regularly on TV, some mums and children choose to watch these together; consequently, childbirth is not the taboo it used to be.. Many Mums tell me that although they maybe didn't plan to watch it with their child, when it came on it was a great discussion starter about the childs own birth.

Sometimes, the mother needs some help and the doctors cut her tummy to lift out the baby; this is called a caesarean birth.

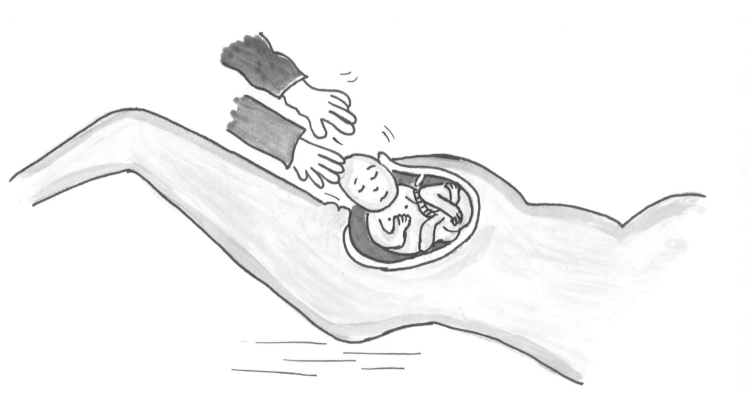

The tube that gave the baby all its food and liquid is then cut. It doesn't hurt the baby; it's like having our hair or nails cut.

The end of the tube on the baby is clipped. The baby is then usually given a big cuddle from its mother or father.

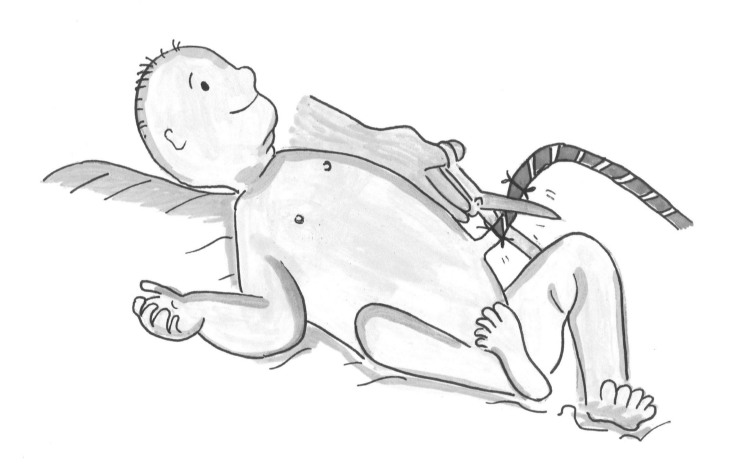

After a few days, the remains of the tube on the baby drop off to leave the belly button. Some people have 'inny' belly buttons and some have 'outies'.

So, now you know more about your body and why it is so important to look after it. Always remember, nobody should touch it unless you want them to.

Many parents and carers worry that if their child knows about their body they will pass on the information to their friends or a teacher. A way to minimise this is to tell your child that they can come and talk to you at any time, but that other parents like to tell their own children themselves. Remember to keep the communication going by perhaps re-capping on the four private areas or using discussion starters via the media or life events.

PG

More simple explanations for four to seven year olds

Topic	Setting	Response
Periods	Often mums tell me their little ones can come toddling into the bathroom and will sometimes catch sight of menstrual blood on a sanitary towel or tampon. This can be quite scary for them as they associate blood with pain ~ think poorly knees. They often question this; don't ignore them but answer:	"Don't worry, it doesn't hurt. Mummy just loses a bit of blood each month; it just shows I'm not having a baby"
Erections	Baby boys are known to have erections even when in the womb. Mothers of boys tell me that spontaneous erections cause lots of giggles and fascination.	"Don't worry; it's your body practising for when you're grown up. You need to look after your body"
Incest	During training sessions with parents they are often shocked when this word comes up in the exercise of 'what to say when'. More are shocked when they realise they have already made reference to it. Young children often say they would like to marry other people in the family when they grow up. We often respond without a second thought.	"We don't marry people in our family when we grow up. You'll probably meet someone new and fall in love with them"
Peer pressure	Children like any other age group can fall victim of peer pressure, whether it's a playground game of "Kiss-Chase" or "you show me yours, and I'll show you mine" in the Wendy House or Home Corner.	"Nobody should make you do things you don't want to do, or touch you when you don't want to be touched. If they do you must tell a parent or teacher".
Girlfriends Boyfriends	Many parents think it's so cute to assign their offspring a boyfriend or girlfriend, in some cases even before they're a year old. This can put children under pressure and can be the cause of teasing and embarrassment. Much better to refer to close friends as...	"A friend that's a boy, or a friend that's a girl"

Topic	Setting	Response
Puberty	Although we may think of puberty as our bodies changing from that of a child to an adult, parents tell me the vast number of two year-olds notice that there are differences. In fact, 'homes with open bathroom door' policies give rise to some wonderful questions, such as: 'what are they?'; 'why do you have hair there?'; 'will mine be as big as that when I grow up?' All of these give a fabulous opportunity to start 'Big Chats'.	"As you get older, your body will start to change and you will gradually get a grown-up body"
Homosexuality	If a child is raised with same sex parents, they will be aware of this from birth, as will children who have gay or lesbian family members or friends. Most schools now have some same sex parents and they are often portrayed in the media, on TV, etc. It is something children will be aware of at a very early age. For a four year-old the simplest way to explain is:	"Sometimes a lady may love another lady, or a man might love another man"

About the Author

Lynnette Smith is a qualified Teacher and Specialist Relationship and Sex Education (RSE) Trainer with a background in youth and community work, having worked in the field since the early 90s. She worked for several Local Authorities and Universities in the Yorkshire and Humber region, before setting up her own business, BigTalk Education in 2005.

Lynnette Smith is the MD and Founder of *BigTalk Education*, she is also the Chair of the Sex Education Forum Advisory Group.

BigTalk Education is a UK based social enterprise who work to ensure as many children and young people as possible receive high quality Relationship and Sex Education. They currently work in 160 schools annually across the country with pupils aged 3 to 18. They also work nationally and internationally with professionals and academics leading the way in the field of relationship and sex education.

Although initially specialising in the delivery of RSE in Secondary Schools, since 2011 Lynnette has spearheaded the *Growing Up Safe: Whole School Approach* Programme, which brings together primary school parents, carers, school staff and pupils working together to keep children safer. The programme has been highly acclaimed, being awarded the Family Planning Association's 2017 Pamela Sheridan award and a finalist for Children & Young People Now's 2018 Safeguarding award. [Winner not yet announced at the time of printing]

To accompany the Programme there are a range of bespoke child friendly resources which have proved successful not only with mainstream primary children, but also those with Special Educational Needs, on the Autism spectrum and children where English is not their first language.

The Government's Women & Equalities Committee (a cross-party select committee) invited Lynnette to Westminster to contribute to a discussion about sexual harassment and assaults in schools. The results of this enquiry were pivotal in RSE becoming statutory as of September 2019. Following this, Lynnette was invited to attend the consultation meeting held by the Department for Education (along with partners such as Public Health England, Barnardo's, Brook, National Children's Bureau, the NSPCC, the National Association of Head Teachers and the Family Planning Association). Lynnette shared her knowledge and experience of age appropriate RSE which contributed to the Department for Education's 2019 statutory RSE guidance.

Lynnette is regularly invited to speak on a variety of Local and National BBC Radio stations and has appeared on Local and National TV, news, documentaries and on current affairs programmes.

Lynnette has two daughters.

For more information on Lynnette please visit
www.bigtalkeducation.co.uk/bigtalk-education/lynnette-smith/

Acknowledgements

My thanks to all the thousands of children and young people who have shared their thoughts, feelings and questions. The Parents and Professionals who have attended the training and shared their experiences, many of whom have given me support and encouragment. The BigTalk Team members past and present who have been so stoic in good and troubled times. Not least, Sharon, Ann, Chloe, Danni and Karl who have always encouraged me.

Lynnette Smith